Handcrafting

Artisan Salves & Lip Balms

From Your Kitchen

Handcrafting

Artisan Salves & Lip Balms

From Your Kitchen

By Alan Bullington

Handcrafting
Artisan Salves & Lip Balms
From Your Kitchen

Published By Alan Bullington
P. O. Box 676
Rogersville, Alabama 35652

ISBN-13: 978-1482374360
ISBN-10: 1482374366

Cover design by Maggie Bullington

Handcrafting
Artisan Salves & Lip Balms
From Your Kitchen

Salves
Salve Making
Essential Oils
Body Butter
Natural Products
Natural Skin Care

"Take not too much of a land, wear not out all the fatness, but leave in it some heart."

Pliny the Elder

Disclaimers

Use all these formulas, recipes and information at your own risk. Herbs and essential oils have a long history of use, but these substances are very powerful and should be used with caution. You could hurt yourself with herbs, so do your own research before using any products on yourself or your family and certainly before selling anything. You're on your own. I am not a trained medical person and make no medicinal claims for any of these products described in this book.

Table Of Contents

1

Introduction

You can quickly put together your own salves and related products. Crafting these items is fun and the result of the effort is something real and useful.

There are some tricks to getting great results. Those tricks, plus all the basics of this craft, are what you get in this book. With the information in this material, you have just what you need to craft professional quality salves and balms.

You can sell what you make too. If you already make another body care product, take what you learn in this book and build a valuable complement to what you now produce. These salves make the perfect addition to soap or candles, for example.

Consider the often overlooked value of the ingredients you can obtain to turn into your salves. Ingredients mentioned here are products of fields, jungles, forests and farms. Such beautful materials all came from plants in one way or another. Most people likely don't even know such cool ingredients as we use are even available.

Coconut oil, beeswax, essential oils and most of the other materials used to make salves did not just drop off a plant!

In most cases someone worked very hard under harsh conditions for low wages to gather the basic materials and to do the initial processing. Usually they worked at this because they had limited opportunities to make money in other ways. That's good for them. We should be thankful for the effort expended by people to get these materials to us in a useable form at an affordable cost.

You get premium salve ingredients at really bargain prices, when you consider all it takes to get them to you and me. Now let's get to it.

2

The Advantages Of Salve Making

After you learn to produce salves, all kinds of opportunities suddenly appear. That's so because the *"salves"* include all sorts of products known by other names. Lip balms, lip gloss, body butters, cuticle creams, skin glaze and the like are all processed just like salves.

You can put low cost luxury products together for yourself, to give as gifts, or to sell. These products are a great value too. A small amount of salve lasts a long time. The added plus of crafting your own products is that you can get as luxurious as you wish, using organic oils or just simple basic ones.

Why Handcrafted Salves?

Salves and balms are ointments applied to the skin, either for healing or just for the soothing feel. They are usually smooth and a little greasy in texture. The greasy feel won't linger though, because the material soaks in. Of course the skin is porous. That means what you put on it goes into your body.

It just makes sense to be very careful about what goes on your skin. This cautious stance has drawn lots of people to these kinds of simpler and more basic products.

Salve products usually contain various herbal preparations, either as essential oils or as herbal infusions. The salve in some cases serves mostly as a carrier for what's in it.

Practitioners of alternative medicine often use salves to correct some skin conditions. Conventional medical practice includes salves too, as carriers for prescription compounds. These products, the salves or whatever they are called, are cheap and readily available or easily formulated.

Have you heard of "drawing salves?" People in the past thought a salve could "draw" out infections along with splinters or other minor irritants. The salves aren't actually drawing anything out, but they do soften the skin around a wound or skin irritation. That softening can and does work irritants out sometimes. So in a way there is some "drawing" happening.

Popular ingredients in such "drawing" salves are ichthammol, as well as bloodroot, calendula, comfrey, arnica and chickweed. By the way, the popular *ichthammol* used in many black salves is an oil shale production byproduct.

The base of many popular store-bought salves is "petrolatum." What is petrolatum? As you might guess, petrolatum is a distilled product from crude oil. Some salve brands with a petrolatum base are Vaseline and Rosebud Salve, among many others.

For well over a hundred years this material, petrolatum, has been applied to skin. Doctors recommend it, at least in some countries. In other places, Europe for example, petrolatum is considered a toxin. Though it is derived from crude oil, the idea is that its highly refined state makes it safe. That is a subject for debate.

Petrolatum based products effectively seal the pores of the skin and prevent moisture loss. That seal prevents the normal breathing of the skin, which is actually a bad thing. Why not skip out on crude-oil-based skin products with your own concoctions?

Why are salves still popular when we have high-tech drugs, creams, medicines and ointments? Realize, of course, that quite a few of these newer compounds are petroleum-based also. The popularity of simpler salve type products is likely because the more natural salves work, at least in some circumstances.

Many people *believe* in the healing power of herbs and simple herbal preparations. It is not unfounded confidence either, since many modern medicines are plant-based, or at least synthetic derivatives of plant compounds. Since there isn't much money for drug companies in herbal salves, there are few, *actually no*, well-funded scientific studies to prove their effectiveness!

Salves soothe skin and moisturize, but in a more fundamental way. Simple moisturizer products with short ingredient lists, indicating a more natural product, with pleasant feel and smells, remain very popular.

These kinds of more basic and simple products are big business too. The salve-type items are key product-lines for several large companies including Burt's Bees, Badger Balm, and Watkins Products. The first two companies were originally built around salve products.

Also quite common are the ads in homestead magazines for healing salves of various sorts. Lately I've seen a "healing chickweed salve" advertised in several different places. Salves and balms are perceived as premium skin care items as well. Especially if formulated from exotic and organic ingredients, salve becomes a luxury item.

Is it tough to produce salves like the ones sold by the millions by these companies? It's not hard at all! It's simple. Since you're not worried about saving a nickel on each container of product you produce, as is the case with big companies, your item you make can be premium and better than what you buy!

Seriously, the cost to use the best ingredients is not that much more than the cost to use cheap ingredients, like petrolatum for example. The cost of organic olive oil is not really that much more than petrolatum, if you only use small quantities.

After I show you how to create salves, you can assemble the ingredients and brew up your own products or give your creations as gifts, or sell some, maybe even start your own business. Our family combined salves with handcrafted soap as a part-time business and sold thousands of containers of salve, at premium prices too! Salves are an easy-to-make product with an "acceptable" profit margin.

Why Not Just Use Lotion?

Why not just stick with lotions? Why bother with salves after all? Here is the reason why. Lotions are oil and water emulsions, or mixtures, whipped so the water and oil stay combined. The problem is this: oil and water emulsions produce the perfect medium for bacteria, mold and fungi to thrive. To stop the resulting undesired growth requires use of an anti-bacterial preservative.

There really is not much way around the preservative. Methyl-paraben, implicated in several health concerns, is the substance of choice for this function. I'll leave it to you to do the health research, but it just seems that anti-bacterial, chemical compounds applied to the skin are not such a great idea. After all, your skin is alive and naturally has bacteria on it and the skin is porous too. What you put on your skin travels right into your body.

What's more, if you look at ingredient lists on skin-care products, you see that lotions often contain propylene glycol which is also used as anti-freeze. This is a questionable material to use for skin-care, at least it is to me and many others. The skin is a membrane that is a path for substances to enter and leave the body. It's used as a delivery pathway for medicines sometimes, as with trans-dermal patches for example.

It makes no sense to assault the body with all kinds of chemicals, even if those chemicals are considered safe by government bodies that evaluate such things.

Some people use lotions containing supposedly beneficial compounds, like MSM, and report positive results from use of such. If the MSM can pass through the skin and have an effect on the body, would the methyl-paraben that is likely in the lotion not enter the body the same way? Of course it would, and so would many of the other chemical concoctions listed on a typical lotion bottle.

Take a look at some lotion bottles. Look at those ingredients and consider how many you recognize. After you do some study on lotion ingredients, you may really question the wisdom of applying lotions to your skin.

For me and my house, with few exceptions, lotions don't seem like a great idea for your health. That's why some people value salve products as a better alternative to lotions. They accomplish the same thing, but permit the user to skip the chemical bath.

The Thing About Lip Balms

The basic formulas for salves and balms make terrific lip balms. However you surely want to use only edible ingredients in what goes near your mouth. At least that's what I want to do.

The instructions in the recipes section show the right sort of formulas for great lip balms. Look for flavor oils especially made for lip balms to add something special. The company Sweet Cakes in the resource section offers a selection of flavor choices for lip balms. Take a look.

Popular lip balms are mostly petrolatum based, so a plant oil based product is quite easy to sell. However lip balms are not usually very expensive, so making a profit selling lip balms is quite difficult.

One way to get around that lack of profit is to offer a container of lip balm that is a little different than the little lip balm tube everybody is accustomed to seeing. Offer a bigger screw-out tube or a pot or tin to justify a little higher price. The cost of a lip balm is in the labor and container cost and not in the balm itself.

Also remember that you are doing people a service when you provide a quality lip balm as substitute for a crude oil based one. Profits aren't everything.

Basic Body Butters

Semi-soft body butters that you can make are just about like lip balms except the proportions of waxes and oils are different. Just getting the proportions right is all it takes to make a desirable butter for skin moisturizing.

As a class of products, the body butters substitute for lotions and do so without subjecting the user to a chemical solution.

Much like lotions, oftentimes the packaging of the "butter" makes or breaks the product.

I can tell you from experience that making up "bars" in molds and then wrapping them in foil for use is NOT a great idea.

What that produces is mostly a mess.

It is far better to put butter bars into tubes with twist-out feeds or pour the mixture in a pot or jar to keep the material in a much easier to use form.

As with lip balms, these simple mixtures of ingredients are sought after and are welcomed as gifts by many.

3

These Are The Basic Ingredients

If there is a simple product to manufacture, it must be salve! Build one of the basic salves by simply combining an oil and beeswax. That's really all there is to it!

Mix oil with beeswax in the proper proportions and you get salve. Beeswax hardens the oils.

You can go about it other ways, like all the salve makers that start with petroleum jelly. A jar of petroleum jelly with a wick inserted does make a nice candle for outside use, though it could be that petroleum jelly doesn't really belong on your skin!

Besides beeswax, one can use other "hardeners," such as carnauba wax, jojoba wax beads, even mango butter or shea butter.

Now, when considering oils to include in your products, it's likely best to just look at plant oils. As suggested, many wish to skip out on the mineral oils and animal products. That rules out lanolin, emu oil, lard and various other animal fats. These have their place, in my opinion, but many people don't think so.

Look mostly at base oils like olive, almond, coconut and so forth. The fun begins as you blend the different oils to get a texture, a consistency, like you want. It's more than just consistency, it's more about the whole package of feel, mosturizing, texture, smell and the overall appeal of the combination of oils. Proper blending and scenting are crucial to producing the best product.

Properties Of Different Oils

Let's look more at oils used in these products. What are the possibilities? Following are several potential oils you can use with just brief comments about the properties of each. Remember, these can be used as a single oil or as a blend. Blending introduces different properties into finished products.

Most of the oils are extracted from nuts and fruit either by mechanical means, pressing of some kind, or by chemical methods, using solvents. If you want to avoid chemicals, you choose the mechanical extraction. Often the extraction method is part of the oil description which you'll see when you're shopping, however sometimes it's in a sort of code. In the descriptions following you will see some ways to tell if you have chemical extracted oils.

Hexane is the most commonly used oil extraction solvent. Why use chemical extraction? It's faster and cheaper than mechanical methods, which rely on heat and pressing. Solvent extraction also recovers more of the oils than can be captured with purely mechanical methods.

Of course the chemical solvents are costly, but the solvents are mostly recovered and reused. Not all is recovered though. The part that remains in the oil is what many consider a health concern. Those concerns are one reason for extraction of oils by purely mechanical means. The good thing is, you have a choice about what you use. Choosing the very best oils is an option to you as the producer.

Consider the following oils as basic to putting salves together for yourself.

Olive – pressed from ripe olives mostly grown around the Mediterranean Sea. Consider extra virgin oil, which results from the first olive pressing. Subsequent pressing produces what is called virgin oil and subsequent solvent extraction produces pure, refined A, and pomace grades. Terminology differs somewhat on some of these.

Olive oil imparts a green tint if used as a major ingredient. These oils possess a somewhat heavy feel and are a bit sticky to the touch. Otherwise, olive oil makes for a wonderful substance for use on the skin.

Coconut – pressed from coconut meat. Like olive oil, first pressings of coconut are referred to as extra virgin. Virgin oils are from the next pressings without chemicals.

Fractionated coconut oil has a completely different water-like consistency and soaks right into the skin. The fractionated oils result after certain fatty acids are removed from the oil. It is, in fact, then a "fraction" of the whole oil. The fractionated oils are used in certain medical applications and in cosmetics.

Refined and solvent extracted 76 and 92 degree coconut oils are most often used in soap and skin care products. The numbers refer to the temperature in Fahrenheit degrees where the oil changes from solid to liquid.

The term "RBD" on coconut oil stands for refined, bleached and deodorized. You can skip those refined oils if you like and go right to the virgin or extra virgin to avoid solvent traces.

Almond – derived from almond pits. Almond oil is an excellent moisturizer often chosen as a massage oil. Sweet almond oil is what you want. Much almond oil is solvent extracted, so you really want the pressed oil produced without chemicals. The pressed oil is often described as "expeller pressed." It results from mechanically pressing the pits.

Avocado – pressed from avocado flesh. The oil from the avocado is considered a healing oil, very moisturizing. It readily penetrates skin and can be purchased as both refined and unrefined.

Macadamia – from macadamia nuts. The oil is very moisturizing. In consistency this oil is much like one's natural skin oil. As such it soaks in quite readily and that makes it useful in cosmetics and in make-up.

Jojoba – a thick, pale yellow liquid extracted from the bean-like seeds of a desert shrub. Jojoba resembles the natural oil, sebum, secreted by the human skin. The waxy oil readily soaks into all skin types.

This wax-like oil does not quickly go rancid and is stable for long periods of time. It's a favorite carrier for essential oils for skin care. Wow, it surely has jumped up in price though. If only used in small amounts price is not such a factor however.

Hemp – extracted from seed of the hemp plant. It is thought to encourage cell growth. Hemp oil is easily absorbed, but without some protection the material tends to spoil relatively quickly. Spoiled, stinking oils are a problem anywhere.

If you look at the resources section, you see that it is easy to get many other oils to use in handcrafted products. You can find cherry kernel oil, apricot kernel oil, peach kernel oil, rice bran oil and many others as well. The ones listed here are basic oils that make great salves.

Note that some people are allergic to nuts and nut oils, even including coconut oil, which is found in all kinds of products. If anyone else is going to use your products, very clearly specify the ingredients.

Of course many people are allergic to ingredients in commercial products too. Probably far fewer people react to the closer-to-nature ingredients, but be careful and considerate.

Consider using only organic oils as a way to build the best products possible. By choosing organic ingredients, you get oils produced under more closely monitored conditions. The oils are also probably processed using less chemical-intensive methods.

It may be that you can then use the oils you obtain for salve making in cooking as well, if you have the high quality oils on hand. That gets you a double benefit, high quality materials for skin care products and the best oils for eating and cooking. Think about it.

Butters For Skin Care

Several buttery products add texture and moisturizing properties to salves. Compared to liquid oils, butters are thicker and more luxurious. When using butters, less wax hardener is required for producing hard, finished products. A smaller quantity of wax in a mix makes a softer, more pliable, less waxy feel. It's the balance of ingredients that produces unique and superior products. There are numerous butters available, but the ones listed here are what you need to get going.

Shea butter – from the fruit of the African Karite tree. You can find this in unrefined form, a smooth paste with a smoky smell and color. In some cases the initial processing is done over open fires. This may explain the smell and color! The refined version is white, almost odorless, and hard. Unrefined has a great feel, but you want to use refined for lip balms to avoid any unpleasant, smoky fire scent in your finished products. Notice the ingredients in European chocolates. Often these better chocolates contain shea butter in the recipe. Check those labels.

Cocoa butter – the solid fat from the roasted seed of the cacao plant. This is valued as a skin lubricant and for its natural cocoa scent, which is almost over-powering in intensity. It's quite hard and thus thickens and hardens whatever you add it to. A little bit goes a long way. From my own observation in talking to a lot of people, cocoa butter is irritating to some people, both in feel and scent.

Mango butter – from the seed kernels of the mango tree. It is also called mango kernel oil. Its texture is very much like shea butter and the material substitutes for shea butter. The mango butter is more creamy textured compared to shea butter, which tends to be a little lumpy, bumpy and gritty.

Many traditional salves include other butter-like materials. As is mentioned elsewhere, the petroleum based "petrolatum" is the basis of many salves. Other substances often used in salves and balms are emu oil and lanolin. Though using the oil found in emus is a little disgusting and so is rubbing sheep wool fat over you, these items all are preferred by some. We think petrolatum, as well as emu oil and lanolin, are a bad idea as skin care ingredients. Better options abound, as you have seen in this section.

Waxes For Skin Care

To get the oil part of a salve to firm up, you add something to make it harden. As already mentioned, that something is wax and the most commonly used wax is beeswax, but it could be other waxes as well. Following are some of those waxes and what they are like.

Beeswax – varies much depending on its source and processing methods. The wax varies in texture, color, purity, and smell. The variation affects your finished product, but maybe not enough to tell. You certainly don't want a lot of trash in the wax, as you get with inadequate filtering. However, virtually all beeswax commercially available is clean. You can choose a cosmetic grade, but that is not a must. Considered a moisturizer, beeswax imparts a slight honey scent and a waxy feel.

Mention beeswax and you naturally think of honey. Putting honey on yourself is bound to be a sticky experience. Surely though, beeswax has some honey in it, or at least it was close to honey at some point. That means when you use beeswax you may be getting some of those healthy benefits that honey furnishes without the mess. Honey is certainly a powerful antiseptic and a real plus for skin troubles.

You might consider buying beeswax in bead form. That way you get little pellets of wax rather than larger, poured, molded chunks. As mentioned elsewhere, cutting hard chunks of wax into smaller pieces puts one's fingers at risk. Cutting up wax is dangerous. The little pellets solve that problem.

Candelilla – derived from a shrub found in northern Mexico and the southwestern United States. This sort of wax is used as a glazing agent in foods and cosmetics and is very hard, brittle and shiny. It substitutes in most ways for beeswax, though it is not as readily available or as affordable. Candelilla wax is often found in lip balms and is sometimes used as a binder in chewing gum.

Carnauba – also called palm wax or Brazil wax since it only comes from certain palm trees found just in northern Brazil. Carnauba wax carries the title "queen of waxes." To harvest the product, the leaves of the special palm trees are collected and dried. The dried leaves are then beat upon to loosen the wax, which is then collected and refined. This material results.

The product gets a grade according to purity, based on the type and extent of filtering. It's used as a thickener in all sorts of cosmetics and skin care preparations because it soothes the skin while adding gloss or shine. The shiny property makes it valuable as a component of car wax, furniture polish, and floor wax as well as dental floss. Carnauba wax is harder than beeswax. Recipes must be adjusted to include less carnauba than you would beeswax.

Jojoba beads – available as wax beads rather than the more common liquid form of jojoba. The hard wax is formed from the liquid wax produced from a plant. The plant that produces the wax is called goat nut, deer nut, pig nut, wild hazel, quinine nut, coffeeberry, and gray box bush. The wax comes from the nut. More like the skin oil and whale oil than vegetable oils, this valuable material deserves a special spot in the salve maker's tool kit.

Any of these waxes make a marvelous addition to salves or balms, but you'll see as you use them that the beeswax is tough to top for the price and what it can do.

If you look at the commercial product ingredients beginning on page 55 and continuing on the following pages, you see that beeswax is really the only wax used. You miss little by just sticking with beeswax as the main hardener in your products.

Using other waxes only produces subtle differences. However you may find that these subtle differences are worth the extra effort and expense in some cases.

Preservatives For Oils

Some oils spoil or go rancid over time. It's mostly the unsaturated oils that "go bad." The unsaturated oils are the ones that are in liquid form at room temperature. That means that coconut oil is not a problem and really neither are palm and jojoba. The butters like shea and mango are not much of a problem either.

Preservatives are mostly for the olive, sunflower, grape seed, apricot kernel, almond, hemp and similar oils that exist as liquids at room temperature. Certainly if you're going to use your salve within six months, you should not require a preservative at all. Otherwise, especially if you're going to sell your creations, you may wish to include a preservative.

Often grapefruit seed extract, also described as citrus seed extract, is used. Grapefruit seed extract is water-soluble however and so it does not combine with oils, and is not worth much as a preservative for the oils. After all, it is the oils going bad, or rancid, that is the concern.

At the present time, rosemary oil extract seems the best choice to preserve oils. It is oil soluble and works well. Water soluble materials mix with water and not with oils. Oil soluble materials combine with oils and not with water. Like the old saying goes, you really can't exactly mix oil and water.

Sometimes vitamin E is used as a preservative, but it is less effective than rosemary oil extract. The vitamin E is certainly an anti-oxidant, but is not particularly effective at preventing rancidity.

The product you want for use as a preservative, or anitoxidant, is *Rosemary Oleoresin Extract* (ROE). Rosemary essential oil is NOT what you want for a preservative.

Get ROE from Glory Bee (see the resources page) as well as from most soap making suppliers.

It only takes a little to get the benefit. Using just 1 part ROE to 2,000 parts oils is all that it takes. That means one drop of Rosemary Oleoresin Extract to 1 ounce (30 ml) of base oil in the product is more than enough.

Beware that ROE smells a lot and it is dark enough to turn light oils a shade of green.

Remember that your main challenge in preserving salves is prevention of rancidity in oils. That means you want an anti-oxidant. It is not really so much a problem of preventing bacteria growth.

Preserving lotions that contain water is an entirely different matter however. As mentioned elsewhere, water and oil emulsions or mixes provide the perfect medium for bacteria growth. That explains the use of preservatives like the parabens in lotions.

Currently there are several alternatives to the parabens. These several alternatives exist in response to health concerns about the parabens used on the skin. One wonders if in time those alternatives will be shown to be worse than the parabens. In any case, the preservatives challenge is different for materials that contain water compared to materials that just use waxes and oils with no water.

In summary, the main concern with long life of salves and balms is prevention of rancidity of the oils in the products. That takes addition of an anti-oxidant.

On the other hand, the trouble with oil and water emulsions, as in lotions, is bacteria, mold, and fungus growth in the product. To prevent this, the maker of these products must include an anti-bacterial preservative. The only way around that is to maintain all those finished products in a properly refrigerated environment, which is not really very practical.

4

Incorporating Herbs Into Products

If nothing else, herbal ingredients impart scents, sometimes very agreeable scents, to salves and balms. Getting the herbs into salves can be accomplished very easily with a minimum of fuss.

You incorporate herbs into oils for use in salves by "infusion." Infusion is the additon of herbs into something else. What you do is add herbal material to oils and then allow the mixture to soak, after which the herbal materials are strained from the liquid and removed. The oil with the "infused" herbal material is then used as an ingredient in salves and balms.

If fresh herbs are used for infusions, water gets introduced into the oils. That water, oil and plant material combination encourages bacteria growth and spoilage. Spoilage within the mix is not a good thing at all, therefore it's essential to use dried herbs. Use only completely dried herbs in your products, if you use herbs at all. Do not use damp or fresh herbs in these infusions.

Even with dried herbs, some moisture can get introduced, with resulting bacteria growth. So refrigeration of the finished salve is recommended if actual herb material is infused into the salves.

More Infusion Details

Herbal infusions can be accomplished in one of the following three ways.

Method 1 – Firstly, to produce an herbal infusion, put ¼ to 1 cup of dried herbs into about 16 ounces of your base oil of choice (see the previous section for oils to use) in a crock-pot or double boiler. Stir. Heat slowly to about 120-130 degrees F. Let the material simmer for an hour or two, stirring occasionally.

After that amount of time, let the mixture cool. Then repeat the heating and cooling process one or two more times. This heating and cooling is referred to as pulsing and this pulls a lot of the herbs into the oil.

Finally, let the mixture cool, but not completely, and strain through several layers of cheesecloth. Squeeze the material in the cloth to get most of the liquid out.

Method 2 – With a second method, simply allow the herbs mixed in the oil to simmer at low heat in the crock-pot for a longer period, perhaps overnight. Skip the pulsing to high and then low temperatures.

Strain out the herbs after the mix is cool. This works well too.

Method 3 – A third method works this way. You place the herb and oil mixture in a pan in a sunny location and just let it stay there for a few days. The heat of the sun does the work. Then after a few days you strain the herb material out, as in the other methods.

Each of these three simple methods works just fine to produce herbal infused oils to use in your salves and balms.

Recommended Herbs

Herbs in endless variety may be added to salves. The following list includes the more common ones, with a brief comment about the traditional use of each.

Calendula – from the marigold family. Helps to soothe inflamed tissues, aids in healing of cuts and abrasions.

Plantain – relieves pain of insect bites and is a remedy for cuts and skin infections.

Comfrey – helps wounds to heal quickly, and used for burns, blisters and inflammation.

Chickweed – cooling antiseptic herb used to treat inflammation and relieve itching, blisters, boils.

St. John's Wort – used for burns, insect bites, wounds, bruises, sores, fungal infections, itching.

These infusions often add color to whatever they are added to as well. That makes for an interesting result sometimes.

Essential Oils For Salves & Balms

Aromatic oils are removed by various extraction processes from plant parts. The oils removed without solvents are called essential oils. On the other hand, the solvent extracted oils are called absolutes. Essential oils are most often used in skin-care products, though all the aromatic oils are used in various ways in the practice of aromatherapy.

Aromatherapy purports to use plant oil extracts to address skin challenges as well as for circulatory, respiratory, and emotional problems. Different oils are used for different purposes. Oils are blended based on combining characteristics of different oils. We'll note some typical uses of different oils, but certainly would not claim any expertise as an aromatherapy expert.

The several methods of oil extraction produce different final products. The most common extraction method is steam distillation. Plant material is placed on a grate above boiling water. The steam passing through the plant material ruptures the cell walls releasing the plant oils. Then the steam passes through a cleanser where it changes into liquid form. The liquid is then separated into the essential oil and plant water, called hydrosol.

On the other hand, some plant materials are processed using mechanical extraction. Citrus peel is an example. The material is squeezed mechanically and then the plant oil is captured. This can be done with heat or without heat.

Absolutes are oils extracted using a petrochemical solvent. Solvent extraction works better than steam processing for delicate materials, flower petals for example. Further processes are used to remove *most* of the solvent. Steam destroys many delicate materials and thus certain solvents are in some cases the only way to get extracts.

There are other methods used to get at the "essential juices," including carbon dioxide extraction and solvent extraction of florasols, but these products would not be used in salves and balms due to costs, if nothing else.

Blending Essential Oils

Though some use essential oils in products for the therapeutic effects, others are satisfied just to get the good aroma of the herbal essences.

Blending for scent, or perfumery, is a rare skill. Most anybody can put together some blends, but not many possess the resources to approach what the perfume industry does. However even a single essential oil produces pleasant smells. Popular single scents are lavender, lemongrass, patchouli and the mints. Combinations of lavender and rosemary are often chosen as a scent blend. Unlike scents used in soap making, in salves and balms one can use more delicate scents like the citrus ones to good effect. It's hard to beat orange and tangerine oils for fresh scents. Using 5-fold orange oil is a good idea in skin products, as it does not cause sensitivity to the sun.

If what you want is the therapeutic effect from essential oils, one can simply combine oils with the desired effect. There exists much accumulated information about the effects of different oils on different conditions. The truth is though that nobody really knows exactly how essential oils work to cure ailments, or maybe they don't work at all.

Common sense dictates that you only use essential oils diluted in carrier oils. Don't use them straight. That's where the salves come in. You can blend essential oils for whatever purpose you have, and then use the salve as a carrier to deliver the oils.

Following are several essential oils with the traditional use of that oil in skin care. This is just a starter as there are endless options to explore.

Bay – scalp tonic
Bergamot – oily skin
Caraway – tissue regeneration
Carrot – reduces wrinkles, improves complexion
Cedar wood – relieves itch, oily skin
Chamomile – for dry skin, skin troubles
Cypress – excess perspiration
Eucalyptus – skin eruptions, wounds
Frankincense – rejuvenation, wrinkles
Geranium – skin tonic, all skin conditions
Hyssop – wounds
Jasmine – dry, sensitive conditions
Juniper – useful for oily skin, cleansing
Lavender – rejuvenator
Lemon – lightens freckles
Lime – greasy skin
Mandarin – cell regeneration
Myrrh – good for mature skin
Neroli – good for all skin types
Palmarosa – wrinkles, for dry skin
Parsley – helps all skin disorders
Patchouli – rejuvenating
Peppermint – all irritations
Pettigrain – for spotty skin
Rosemary – skin tonic
Sandalwood – good for all skin types
Tea tree – for all irritations
Thyme – skin tonic
Ylang – for face and oily skin

5

Building These Products

Mixing up salves is really as easy as combining your oils and beeswax and melting it. There are several refinements and best ways to go about it.

To get started here is a list of what it takes to mix up the products. Following the list are the salve building steps, and then some tips to get the best results.

1. Double boiler or Pyrex beaker and sauce pan
2. A scale to measure ingredient weights
3. Stirring spoons
4. Candy thermometer
5. Cutting board
6. Beeswax cutter (see below tips)
7. Molds for the product (could actually be the final containers)
8. Storage container for finished products

Step 1 – Weigh your ingredients. You can skip the scales and just use volumes to make salves. This is a bad idea. It is very difficult to get a volume for the unmelted waxes. By using a scale you add accuracy to your measurements, making it much easier to get exact results and consistent product each time you make a batch. Don't try this without a scale.

Step 2 – Now add the beeswax pieces to your oils and heat in a double boiler. Alternatively, you can heat in a Pyrex beaker in a pan of water over medium heat, propping the beaker up with a jar lid so it's not flat on the bottom of the pan. Using the Pyrex beaker is actually simpler, as the beaker is relatively easy to use to pour the oil mix from after the mixing and processing is complete.

Overheating a glass container could cause it to break. You must monitor and moderate the temperature change. Use a candy thermometer in the ingredients to maintain control. Temperature should be limited to no more than 170 degrees F. Do not include scent oils yet. The scent oils go in as part of Step 4.

Step 3 – The next step is critical and a little tricky. If you use shea butter in your blend, the temperature of the mix is important.

If the temperature isn't right, shea butter, if melted and then allowed to harden again, will be gritty. You won't like the resulting salve. It's almost scratchy.

To avoid this, maintain the ingredients at about 170 degrees F for about 15 minutes if shea butter is included in the mix. This step eliminates the fat crystals that cause grittiness. It's that simple.

You maintain elevated heat long enough to melt the beeswax. Afterwards remove the container from the heat. Let the mix cool for just a few minutes.

Shea butter works very well in salves and balms. It just takes that little extra step to eliminate an undesired texture.

Step 4 – Add scent oils and other additives, like preservatives, only after all other heating has happened. Overheating the essential oils is a good way to lose those oils and basically boil them away. That's a waste that should be avoided.

Put the essential oils in at the last possible point. The temperature must stay elevated however or the wax will harden on you. You'll see how that goes with experience.

Step 5 – Now pour the melted mixture of oils, waxes and additives into your prepared molds. Allow the mixture to cool and the mix hardens. If your mix starts to harden before you finish, just heat it a little to turn everything back to a liquid state and then resume pouring.

Step 6 – Some tweaking provides for seasonal changes and climate variation. In very hot and dry weather, you need more hardness compared to what's needed in very cold conditions. Use a little higher proportion of beeswax, or the other hardeners, to adjust for warmer weather.

Now consider these related tips that go along with the above steps.

* Tip 1 - Beeswax is tough to melt. Grate it or cut it in small pieces to speed things along. Be careful when you cut the wax though, because beeswax is truly very hard. If you go at the wax with a knife, you can easily carve on yourself and produce serious injuries! Here are suggestions for getting beeswax cut into pieces.

1. Heat a knife with hot water to make cutting through the block easier.
2. Put the wax in the freezer overnight. Afterwards put the wax in a cloth bag and on a

hard surface and whack it with a hammer! Select from the pieces.

3. Use a bandsaw on the block.

4. Use a wood chisel and a hammer to break off small pieces.

5. Use a cheese grater!

As you can see from these suggestions, dealing with this hard wax is quite difficult. It can be done though. Actually I've always split off pieces with a heavy knife. You really have to be careful though.

* **Tip 2** - It is possible to burn the oils, even to catch them on fire. We don't want that. So you must monitor the temperature while you heat oils and stir occasionally.

* **Tip 3** - Just to emphasize, you can infuse any of the herbs into the oils used to make salves. So for any of the recipes that follow, use the infusion directions to make whatever type of salve you want.

* **Tip 4** - It's as much the oils and beeswax that make the salve useful, as it is any herbs or additives. Certainly proper combinations of oils and beeswax make for a more satisfactory salve.

6

Proven Recipes For Salves & Balms

Several recipes follow. As you will see, these are all variations on the salve theme. Most are mixtures of oils, butters and waxes in different proportions. The varied proportions produce varied results.

Some of these recipes show weights that are tweaked to get them just right. Some are more general.

In every case if you want a larger or smaller recipe batch, simply multiply the amount given by whatever proportion you wish to scale the recipe up or down. Multiply each ingredient amount by 2 to double the batch size or by ½ to cut the batch size in half. It's that simple.

If you mix up a batch of salve and the mix is too soft or too hard, just remelt it and add oil or add beeswax to change it like you want. Add oil to make it softer or add beeswax or your other waxes to make it harder.

Keep a written record of what you do and next time you can get it just right the first time! This sort of tweaking is required, as different climates and temperatures require slightly different proportions of waxes and oils. Keeping careful records makes it easy to really invent unique products that are your very own. Just get yourself a little notebook and start from the beginning of your efforts to record what you do as you build each batch and soon you will have a valuable resource as you continue to alter and improve your products.

After you put together a few batches of material, you begin to see how simple it is to devise your own recipes. Substitute one wax for another, one base oil for another and then you can substitute a buttery fat for another fat.

That substitution and variation opens up endless possibilities for new products. These possibilities result simply from varying proportions of the ingredients in a salve or balm recipe. That kind of variation just produces differences in the base salve, balm or butter. Varying the herbal additives opens up even more possibilities.

Remember that all the oils called for in these recipes can be infused with herbs as desired. The herb infused oil works in any of these recipes.

Now on to the base recipes. Remember these are simply the starting points. The real key to product development is to make changes to these and develop your own recipes.

Glaze For Glow

Beeswax	25 grams
Carnauba Wax	10 grams
Jojoba Beads	25 grams
Fractionated Coconut Oil	250 grams
Mango Butter	25 grams
Vitamin E	5000 IU
Scent	1 ¼ teaspoons

Packaged in tiny pots. This blend produces premium look and feel. Note that the jojoba is in waxy bead form here and not liquid. You're getting some hardness and "shine" from the combination of beeswax, carnauba wax and the jojoba beads. This is really a different sort of luxury item.

This has been described by some as "my favorite" of all these products.

See how you could easily substitute refined shea butter for the mango butter. You could leave off the carnauba wax and increase the quantity of jojoba beads and get about the same result. In each case it would take some slight modifications to the ratio of oils and waxes to get a resulting product with the exact same feel.

Modifying these recipes to get slightly different results makes building these products a lot of fun. Slight changes will get you a little bit different result. The possibilities are endless. That's for sure.

Lightly Lavender Ointment

Beeswax	5 grams
Carnauba Wax	2 grams
Jojoba Beads	5 grams
Fractionated Coconut Oil	50 grams
Mango Butter	5 grams
Vitamin E	1000 IU
Bulgarian Lavender Essential Oil	25 drops

This is the same recipe as the "Glaze For Glow." This illustrates changing recipe batch size and specifying a scent. Note also that for marketing purposes just changing the name makes it appear as a completely different product. In a way changing essential oils in the recipe *does* make it a different product.

All I did to convert "Glaze For Glow" to this one is divide each quantity by 5 and then add the scent. I had to know how many drops were in a teaspoon, as the original recipe called for teaspoons for the scent. I just looked up the conversion in the table in the Resources And Ideas section. A teaspoon is 100 drops so I made the conversion of 1¼ teaspoons to 125 drops. Dividing by 5, as for all the quantities, gave a result of 25 drops. That's the source of the 25 drops of Bulgarian Lavender Essential Oil.

Super Simple Shea Salve

Shea Butter   99%
Jojoba Oil   1%

Use just enough jojoba oil to soften your shea butter. The amount needed depends on the type and source of the shea butter. Note that melting the mix, as described in Chapter 5, step 3, eliminates any gritty feel from the shea butter. The addition of the oil changes the whole nature of the butter into a much more easy-to-use and luxury-feel product.

Aging Skin Super Simple Shea Salve

Shea Butter   99 grams
Jojoba Oil   1 gram
Lavender Essential Oil   9 drops
Neroli Essential Oil   9 drops
Myrrh Essential Oil   6 drops

This is simply an example of the Super Simple Shea Salve with quantities inserted. Melt the shea butter and jojojba oil together. Maintain the mixture at about 170 degrees F for 15 minutes. Let it cool slightly and then add the essential oils and pour into containers. These essential oils were chosen from the table in the Resources And Ideas section on page 69.

All Time Best Lip Balm

Beeswax	150 grams
Shea Butter (Refined)	290 grams
Macadamia Nut Oil	236 grams
Jojoba Oil	75 grams

Scent (Your Choice):	
5 Fold Orange Essential Oil	5 ¼ teaspoons **OR**
Peppermint Essential Oil	1 teaspoon **OR**
Lavender Essential Oil	½ teaspoon

We put this exact mix in ¾ ounce lotion tubes, like big lip balm tubes, and marketed this as a lip balm or convenient portable spot moisturizer. The measurements reflect tweaking to get the consistency just right.

Remember that refined shea butter should be heated to 170 degrees F and maintained at that temperature for 15 minutes to make sure the gritty particles are all melted. You accomplish that by melting all the oils and beeswax together and then holding the temperature of the mix at the 170 degrees F for the 15 minutes. Only then should you add the essential oils. Allowing the mixture to cool a bit before adding essential oils is even better.

Adding flavor oils to taste makes this even better.

Luxury Lotion Bar

Beeswax	125 grams
Shea Butter	210 grams
Macadamia Oil	140 grams
Jojoba Oil	25 grams

Scent:

Bitter Almond Essential Oil	2 teaspoons **plus**
Tea Tree Essential Oil	½ teaspoon **plus**
Peru Balsam EssentialOil	½ teaspoon

We sold this mixture in a "deodorant tube" to be used as a lotion bar. That makes the material convenient to use, but not messy. Pour in a mold to make whatever size and shape is desired.

Here is an example of using the tea tree oil for scent and skin healing properties, but you would *NOT* put tea tree oil in a lip balm. If you do then you get burned lips and a bad taste. You would not want bitter almond essential oil in the lip balm either.

The Tea Tree Herbal Salve

Olive Oil	2 cups
Beeswax	1 ounce
Tea Tree Essential Oil	8 drops
Lavender Essential Oil	8 drops
Vitamin E	400 IU

This is much lighter in texture than the previous mixes, almost liquid. Put this salve in a pot or tin!

Consider infusing dried calendula flowers into the olive oil for superior results. Remember to strain out the flowers before using the oil!

That Lotion Stick Solution

Cocoa Butter	170 grams
Sweet Almond Oil	206 grams
Beeswax	134 grams
Vitamin E	4 drops
Lavender Essential Oil	2 teaspoons
Rosemary Oleoresin Extract	10 drops

This mixture illustrates the use of rosemary oleoresin extract as an antioxidant. Rosemary oleoresin extract is not suitable for lip balms as the taste is unpleasant. Here we use cocoa butter instead of shea butter. This gives the blend a different smell and texture.

Very Best Herbal Deodorant

Beeswax	1 ½ Tablespoons
Cocoa Butter	½ Tablespoon
Coconut Oil	1 Tablespoon
White Thyme Essential Oil	15 drops
Rosemary Essential Oil	15 drops
Lavender Essential Oil	25 drops

Very similar to the other products, but with essential oils chosen as deodorizers. Note that this little recipe just produces a tiny amount. Unlike the other recipes, this one shows volume amounts and not weights. This makes it easy to put together with no scale. To refine this recipe you likely want to use the chart on page 67 and substitute weights for these volumes. That calculation produces the following amounts.

Beeswax	21 grams	(1 ½ Tablespoons)
Cocoa Butter	7 grams	(½ Tablespoon)
Coconut Oil	14 grams	(1 Tablespoon)
White Thyme Essential Oil		15 drops
Rosemary Essential Oil		15 drops
Lavender Essential Oil		25 drops

Ultimate Lip Balm & Solid Lotion

Beeswax	20 grams
Shea Butter	35 grams
Sweet Almond Oil	45 grams

A simple blend we've used. Many recipes show 1/3 beeswax, 1/3 shea butter and 1/3 almond oil. That produces a very hard product. This ratio is better. Getting the ratio of beeswax to oils correct makes all the difference in the feel of these kinds of products.

One Cool Basic Light Salve

Beeswax	10 grams
Olive Oil	90 grams
Rosemary Oleoresin Extract (optional)	2 drops
Essential Oils (optional)	30 drops

A very basic salve using just enough beeswax to harden the oil and then adding essential oils of your choice. Choose essential oils from the chart in the Resources And Ideas section or just pick whatever you like.

7

Different Applications

Salves are marketed either as an alternative to more conventional products or for skin or health related benefits. For an example of the first type, "natural" lip balms are clearly an alternative to petroleum-based lip balms. Examples of salves with claimed health related benefits are the poison ivy creams and fungus remedies, both just salves tailored with additives for a specific purpose.

Below are ingredient labels copied from several commercially available salve products. See what the product is called and then note the ingredients.

Each is simply a blend of oils and wax with variations on that basic theme. Note the creative use of "flower essence" in the first example. That's beeswax.

Tea Tree Lavender Salve – Olive oil extracts of chickweed, halva and plantain with essential oils of tea tree and lavender and flower essence.

Watkins – Canola oil, sweet almond oil, beeswax, lavender oil, vitamin E, chamomile oil, and eucalyptus oil.

Burt's Bees Lip Balm – Beeswax, coconut oil, sunflower oil, tocopheryl acetate and tocopheryl, lanolin, peppermint oil, comfrey root extract, rosemary extract.

Badger Balm – Certified organic extra virgin olive oil, natural beeswax, castor oil, organic aloe vera extract, also essential oil.

Face Cream – Grape seed oil, apricot kernel oil, coconut oil, cocoa butter, aloe vera gel and juice, lanolin, beeswax, essential oils of vanilla and sandalwood.

Chickweed Healing Salve – Chickweed, comfrey, mint, olive oil, beeswax, lavender, rosemary and eucalyptus.

Take a look at a selection of salve products and you will see the same pattern. Studying labels on these products is a fun project, especially after you realize how easy it is to put these together yourself.

8

Marketing

If you choose to sell your products, you can go about marketing them in several ways. Salves are nostalgic and simple products that are familiar to many people.

On a small scale, probably your best chance for selling is when you can explain face-to-face what you have to a potential costumer. Here are possible places to do just that:

1. Farmer's markets
2. Craft fairs
3. Art shows
4. Street festivals
5. School sponsored events
6. Harvest festivals
7. Rennaisance fairs
8. Trade shows
9. Historical reenactments

One of the major advantages of these events may not be so clear. In every case when you are part of one of these events, you can put what you have to sell in front of a *lot* of people in a relatively short period of time. That means you can potentially make many sales quickly and with minimum expenditure of time or money. Many ways to sell products require large investments of time or money. These events take neither.

Then when you make some sales, you offer ways for your customer to easily get more of what they bought, plus other items as well. It's that ability to generate follow-up sales that makes these kinds of small business ventures a possible way to really get something going. Repeat business makes it work too.

Besides face-to-face selling, gift shops are possible marketing outlets. Additionally, herb shops, health food stores, or even tourist destinations with outdoor attractions offer more places to sell what you make. Your display must be attractive and well designed. Actually when you think about it, almost any check-out counter is a potential location for salves. Even auto parts stores carry Badger Balm.

Salves can be a stand-alone product or will combine well with other items for marketing. Soap, for example, is the perfect complement to salves, as are candles or herbal sachets. Giving special discounts for purchasing multiple items is one way to generate more sales.

Simple marketing materials make it easier to get repeat sales. Those materials include a simple print brochure, well-designed product labels, as well as the right kind of business cards. All must point toward easy ways to get more of what you have to offer.

Certainly the internet offers a chance to sell salves too. At the simplest level, a website is like an online brochure performing a similar function to your paper brochure.

Your own website makes it simpler to get follow-up sales from buyers that you find from your "off-line" activities.

There are so many ways to get a website up and going that the possibilities are limitless and extremely confusing. Even more confusing is how you can get anybody to a site to actually see what you have to offer.

At this point one of the simplest site builders to set up a site for selling products, like what you can make if you actually use this information, is at http://www.clevergizmos.com. What you get there is a simple WordPress based theme that easily ties to a payment processor with no need for a merchant account. The Internet is so fast changing that this method of site building may not be best for long.

The best way to get traffic to a website and get some eyes on your offer is another changing target. The more places that reference or mention your products, the better your chances for making some sales. These "backlinks," which is what a reference to your site from another site is called, are part of the key to getting your page found.

Here are a few of the places to spread the word about your page.

1. Article directories
2. Press releases
3. Video sites
4. Social sites like Twitter, Facebook
5. Special case sites like Squidoo, InfoBarrel
6. Forum posts
7. Your own blogs
8. Guest articles on other blogs
9. Paid ads

There are all sorts of ways to get some attention to a product sales page and these are just a few. What works best is a moving target. It's better to let the link building happen naturally, but some promotion plan is likely a must.

In addition to your own site, it is a fairly simple matter to get products up on Etsy or eBay or Amazon. These all have traffic of their own, but all work better with some promotion from elsewhere too.

Marketing on the web is in many ways more risky and tougher than more conventional and traditional approaches. The barriers to entry are quite small, but the competition in most areas is beyond fierce. What it takes to get traffic is constantly evolving. If you decide to give selling online a try, be ready for the challenge of a lifetime. It may be worth the effort.

Containers

Salves and balms are used for a variety of purposes and appeal to many groups. Just a few examples of different products follow with different potential market groups.

Lip Balm

1. Conventional plastic tube, the twist to advance type, like a lipstick tube, for most users
2. Conventional plastic pot for those who prefer that container
3. Glass pot – for those who don't like plastic
4. Metal pot – light and non plastic

General Moisturizing

1. Body butter – form in small soap molds and simply wrap with foil
2. Plastic "deodorant tube"
3. Glass jar
4. Metal pots
5. Plastic pots
6. Various size plastic tubes with the "twist to advance" feature

Deodorant

1. Plastic deodorant tubes
2. Glass or tin pots

If you decide to make some products to sell, the same ingredients in a different container will appeal to totally different markets.

I prefer glass or metal containers to plastic and so do many others. Some people would choose a colorful plastic container however. Pick what you prefer and what your customers want if you're going to sell your products.

9

Resources And Ideas

Following are our tried and tested best sources for salve and balm making supplies.

Base Oils

Columbus Foods Company
730 N. Albany Avenue, Chicago, IL 60612
www.columbusfoods.com 800-322-6457
Just oils, butters, and waxes. Tremendous selection, great prices and service.

Rainbow Meadow, Inc.
4494 Brooklyn Road, Jackson, MI 49201
www.rainbowmeadow.com 517-764-9765
Excellent selection of supplies including base oils, essential oils and molds.

Essential Oils

Liberty Natural Products
SE Stark Street, Portland, OR 97215
www.libertynatural.com 800-289-8427
Wholesale prices on huge selection of essential oils, additives, packaging and other products. Great!

Herbal Additives

Ameriherb
P. O. Box 1968, Ames, IA 50010-1968
www.ameriherb.com 800-267-6141
Huge selection of herbs, spices, plant materials. Rock bottom prices. Must-have catalog.

Healing Spirits Herb Farm
61247 Rt 415, Avoca, NY 14809
www.healingspiritsherbfarm.com 607-566-2701
Check these folks out. They have the most beautiful dried herbs.

Other Stuff

GloryBee Foods, Inc.
120 N. Seneca Road, Eugene, OR 97402
www.glorybeefoods.com 800-456-7923
Specializes in bee products, but has a great selection of supplies including molds, oils and hardware.

Sweet Cakes
www.sweetcakes.com 952-945-9900
Flavors for lip balms.

Packaging

Sunburst Bottle Company
4500 Beloit Drive, Sacramento, CA 95838
www.sunburstbottle.com 916-929-4500
All kinds of bottles.

Lavender Lane Forever
P. O. Box 600, Merlin, OR 97532
www.lavenderlane.com 541-474-3551
Glassware plus essential oils and other supplies.

Federal Packaging Network
4044 Peavey Road, Chaska, MN 55318-2344
www.federalpackage.com 952-448-7900
Wholesale source for large quantities of a variety of tubes and packaging.

Uline
2200 S. Lakeside Drive, Waukegan, IL 60085
www.uline.com 800-295-5510
Good source for shipping material and many kinds of packaging.

Labels

Grower's Discount Labels
P. O. Box 70, 632 Tunnel Road, Tunnel, NY 13848
www.growersdiscountlabels.com 800-693-1572
Custom labels including design and printing. Small business, terrific service.

Online Labels
www.onlinelabels.com 888-575-2235
Big selection of blank labels at huge discounts.

Regulations

Salves fall under the cosmetics category of federal regulations in the United States. You may read the regulations on-line. If you sell these products, you fall under these laws. Lucky you.

Actually, many of the guidelines are voluntary. There are several specific requirements for labeling and packaging. Check out the requirements at the link below.

Title 21,
Code of Federal Regulations Cosmetic Products
www.fda.gov/Cosmetics/default.htm

Salve Examples

www.badgerbalm.com
www.burtsbees.com
www.mountainroseherbs.com

Conversions

Metric Volume	U.S. Volume	Metric Weight	U.S. Weight	Metric Volume	Drops**
1 ml	1/5 tsp	0.945 gm		1 cc	20
5ml	1 tsp	4.725 gm	1/6 oz	5 cc	100
15 ml	1 Tbs	14.18 gm	1/2 oz	15 cc	300
30 ml	1/8 cup	28.35 gm	1 oz	30 cc	600

** Drops vary according to dropper.

454 grams = 1 pound

ml = milliliter

tsp = teaspoon

Tbs = tablespoon

gm = grams

oz = ounces

cc = cubiccentimeters

See Rainbow Meadow catalog for good tables.

Essential Oils And Skin Conditions

Following are some potential blends of essential oils for various skin conditions. These are, of course, just based on the traditional use of the particular oils.

These listings are for the number of drops in about 30 grams of salve **or** roughly 30 milliliters, or about 1 ounce, of a carrier oil like jojoba.

In other words, you can put the specified number of drops with about one ounce of jojoba oil in a bottle and you have a product that some people would sell for major money as a remedy for a certain condition.

You could also just mix a blend up and try it for yourself and see what you think.

Making medicinal claims is surely something I refuse to get into and likely you should stay away from as much as possible. If you make any medicinal claims for a product, then that product is treated as a drug! That's not good.

With that in mind, here are some blends to consider based on traditional use of these particular oils.

Acne		**Scarring**	
Chamomile	5	Lavender	5
Bergamot	5	Chamomile	5
Pine	3	Frankincense	4

Acne		**Aging Skin**	
Tea Tree	5	Lavender	3
Juniper	4	Neroli	3
Petitgrain	3	Myrrh	2

Acne		**Melanosis**	
Tea Tree	4	Neroli	2
Lavender	4	Lemon	1
Bergamot	4	Chamomile	3

Blemishes		**Oily Skin**	
Chamomile	4	Bergamot	2
Geranium	3	Cedarwood	2
Carrot	3	Geranium	1

Exzema		**Dry Skin**	
Chamomile	4	Sandalwood	3
Sandalwood	3	Rosewood	2
Lavender	3	Geranium	1

Scarring		**Wrinkles**	
Lavender	6	Carrot	2
Frankincense	5	Neroli	1
Neroli	3	Frankincense	2

CPSIA information can be obtained at www.ICGtesting.com
Printed in the USA
BVOW08s1206160614

356493BV00021B/944/P

9 781482 374360